S0-BLH-689

Grow Your Key Talent

Thought-Provoking Essays for
Business Owners, Executives & Managers
on Developing Star Staff

Enjoy growing your key talent!

Rebecca Morgan

Rebecca L. Morgan, CSP, CMC

Grow Your Key Talent: Thought-Provoking Essays for Business Owners, Executives and Managers on Developing Star Staff

© 2009 All rights reserved. No part of this book may be reproduced or transmitted in any form or by any means, electronic or mechanical, including photocopying, recording, or by any information storage or retrieval system, without the written permission from the copyright holder, except for the inclusion of quotations in a review.

Printed in the United States of America.

ISBN eBook: 978-1-930039-51-3

printed book: 978-1-930039-27-8

How to order:

Quantity copies may be ordered directly from www.RebeccaMorgan.com.

Visit us online for updates and additional articles.

This book is dedicated to all the CEOs, executives, managers and indi- vidual contributors who know that developing themselves and their staff is the key to success.

Books by Rebecca Morgan

Books

▲ *Calming Upset Customers*

▲ *Grow Your Key Talent: Thought-Provoking Essays for Business Owners, Executives and Managers on Developing Star Staff*

▲ *Inspiring Others to Win*

▲ *Life's Lessons: Insights and Information for a Richer Life*

▲ *Professional Selling: Practical Secrets for Successful Sales*

▲ *Remarkable Customer Service ... and Disservice: Case Studies and Discussions to Increase Your Customers' Delight*

▲ *TurboTime: Maximizing Your Results Through Technology*

MP3s

▲ *Making Time Work For You*

▲ *Recipe for Customer Service Success*

All can be ordered at www.RebeccaMorgan.com

Contents

Introduction

This book is designed for anyone who is interested in improving their organization's results.

Performance improvement does not always have immediately identifiable results. Return on Investment can be hard to measure. But just like a new exercise regime, you know you have to have faith that it will make a difference even when you can't see changes quickly.

How to use this book

You can use this book several ways:

▲ **Refine your management practices:** Read each essay and decide how you can integrate the lessons into your own management practices and your organization's processes.

▲ **Team improvement:** Make sure each team member has his/her own copy. Then assign specific pages to read before a staff meeting and discuss the main points. Get ideas on how your organization and/or each team member can utilize the lessons. Ask each to make a commitment to improve one behavior as a result of the discussion.

▲ ***Individual team member improvement:*** If a staff person is having difficulty understanding why professional development is important, ask him/her to read specific essays you think closely parallel this staff person's challenges. Then meet together to discuss the essay and what s/he learned from it.

We welcome your sharing your ideas, suggestions, and your case studies for future volumes.

About the Author

Morgan Seminar Group is an internationally recognized consulting, training and development firm, based in San José, CA. Founded by Rebecca L. Morgan in 1980, Morgan Seminar Group partners with clients to create innovative, long-lasting professional development solutions. Our focus is strategic customer service, and increasing people-productivity by providing the right skills for the right people in the right way.

Many recognizable organizations have engaged Rebecca to develop creative solutions to their situations. These include: Apple Computer, Singapore Airlines, Wells Fargo Bank, New York Life Insurance, Microsoft, ING, Hewlett-Packard, Adobe, Applied Materials, Quantum, Seagate, Sun Microsystems, Lockheed Martin, Sony, and Stanford University, among many, many more.

Rebecca L. Morgan, Founder and Principal

Morgan Seminar Group founder and principal, Rebecca Morgan, is one of America's most respected and sought-after customer service experts, professional development consultants, authors and speakers. Her media appearances include 60 Minutes, The Oprah Winfrey Show, National Public Radio's Market Place, *USA Today, Wall Street Journal, San José Mercury News,* Malaysia's *Star* newspaper, Singapore's *Straight Times* and the San Francisco Chronicle. Her ideas are so solid, last year Microsoft hired her as their workplace effectiveness spokesperson.

Rebecca's books, recordings, videos and learning tools exemplify the excellence she creates in all of her work. She's authored four popular books — two have been translated into nine languages. Additionally, she's co-authored four others; one is a fund-raiser for the US Olympic team. Her books include: *Calming Upset Customers, TurboTime: Maximizing Your Results Through Technology, Professional Selling: Practical Secrets for Successful Sales,* and *Life's Lessons: Insights and Information for a Richer Life.*

One of an Elite Few Professionals

Rebecca is committed to continuous learning and growing, especially since that is what she imparts to others. She has demonstrated this striving by receiving the Certified Speaking Professional (CSP) designation conferred by the National Speakers Association (NSA). At the time, the ten-year-old designation had been earned by only 215 people in the world—less than seven percent of the 3700 members of NSA.

The CSP is a designation of achievement earned through proven speaking experience. It is awarded to individuals who have completed a comprehensive application process and met NSA's stringent criteria.

She has also earned the professional designation Certified Management Consultant (CMC) from the Institute of Management Consultants (IMC). She is the fifteenth professional in the world to earn both the CSP and the CMC designations.

Candidates for the CMC undergo a thorough investigation of their consulting experience. They are interviewed by a panel of senior consultants to verify their competence. Additionally, candidates must pass a written examination demonstrating their knowledge of the IMC's Code of Ethics.

Developing your managers isn't at the top of the priority list right now.

But it should be.

Kill Your Business by Ignoring This

Another key employee has just quit. When asked why, he states that, among other reasons, his manager was hard to get along with, gave conflicting priorities, and was unavailable for clarification. Additionally, he could be moody, and snap when a staff member made a minor mistake. This isn't the first time you've heard reports like this, not only about this manager, but about several others. You've given them feedback, but they don't seem to change.

That's the least of your worries right now. You've got several big proposals out, and you need to be involved with closing them. You just won several new contracts that require your adding head count, as your people are now stretched too thin. You want to refinance a loan so you can get a better rate and add some much-needed equipment. So developing your managers isn't at the top of the priority list right now.

But it should be.

According to a recent Gallup poll, the top reason employees leave is because of their boss. How much is turnover costing you? How long and how much money does it cost to recruit new people, train them and get them productive? Longer than you'd like.

How long and how much money would it take to fine-tune the skills of your present managers? A lot less than putting out personnel fires, loss of productivity from unhappy workers, and the headaches these cost your senior team and you. What if your managers were better skilled at working with their people so there were fewer problems, higher output, and everyone could focus on doing their jobs, rather than backbiting?

In my nearly 30 years in the people-development business, I've noticed an interesting phenomenon. CEOs and senior staff put off the non-urgent, yet important, task of developing their key talent. I see it much like losing weight. If someone is overweight, it is bothersome. He knows he should do something about it, it's not healthy, and he doesn't look and feel as good as he'd like. Yet it takes a plan, some effort, time and usually some money. It's just easier to live with it, even if he has trouble climbing stairs, finding attractive clothes, feeling good about himself. "It's a lot of trouble," he might say. Or "I know I need a plan, but it has to be one that fits for me, and I don't have time right now to figure it out."

And if he does nothing it will kill him.

Same with developing your key talent.

If you do nothing, the dysfunctionality of your people will kill your business.

So what to do? Here are some ideas (a plan!) to get you started:

▲ Understand the seriousness and ramifications of your doing nothing. Yes, you can continue to skate by for a while. But how long have you been skating by already? Are you close to a major meltdown and don't know it? When it comes, it will take much more time and money — and headaches — than you imagined.

▲ Realize it will take some time and effort on your part to start an effective program. Sustainable progress is not about sending managers to one-day courses, which creates no change. This, like the weight loss plan, needs to be an ongoing effort, not just an every once in a while activity when you can fit it in. It needs to be a well-thought-through plan, with regular learning activities.

▲ Work with an internal or external professional learning consultant who understands how long-term change happens and designs a plan that will ensure measurable results. People learn differently, and may need different learning vehicles for various scenarios. For example, if needing a brush up on interviewing new hires, a book or eLearning may be sufficient. If a manager needs to be better at giving feedback, role playing may be the best solution, whether that's one-on-one with a mentor/coach, or in a class. If there's an issue with not delegating, then a weekly accountability partner may do the trick. The point is to develop a plan with some options beyond a short-term training class to help instill new habits.

▲ Develop accountabilities. All learners need to have accountability to be the most effective. In our weight loss metaphor, the programs that are most effective helping people lose weight are those that have a regular weigh in. That's accountability! Your people need to be accountable to whomever they report to. The accountability is not just for participating in the learning activity ("Yes, I went to class." "Yes, I had my coaching session."). They need to be accountable for taking action on their learnings. It's too easy to attend a learning activity and not change one thing. The learner needs to be accountable for the needed changes, and that accountability needs to be to their boss, not the instructor or HR Department.

▲ Start something, even if the plan is not fully fleshed out. Yes, it would be great if all of the pieces of the puzzle were in place before you begin. Yet, if 80%-90% of the plan is in place, begin with gusto! Development is a dynamic animal. You will be tweaking and modifying it as you go along. Your people will come up with ideas of what they want added and changed to make it even more effective for them. Be flexible.

You may be saying "My people aren't dysfunctional." Great! But do they have the skills to step up to the next level of responsibility? Are they regularly growing and learning how to be better at their job? The same Gallup poll found that one of the reasons top employees leave is if they felt they were not learning and growing, and that no one took an interest in their development.

Don't let the lack of developing your key talent drive away your best people and kill your business. Don't put it off any longer. A crisis may be right around the corner.

Executives want to know how to best maximize their investment in growing their people.

Six Top Questions Leaders Ask About Developing Their Key Talent

Speaking to leaders I've learned that they want to know how to best develop their key staff members. The most common solution they know is to send folks to 1- to 3-day training sessions, or to conferences. They know those get minimal, if any, return on the time and money invested, but they're not clear what other options are available which would have a higher, and longer-term ROI.

They want to know how to best maximize their investment in growing their people. They ask excellent questions. Here are six of the best frequently asked questions, along with my responses.

1. *How can I discern the good training brochures and proposals?*

In the program description, look at the objectives, "this program is for you if…" and/or "at the end of this program, you will be able to…" and determine if that fits your target person/group.

Does the program provider offer any pre-assessment to determine if the session would be valuable or your target person/group? (Many computer classes offer at least a rudimentary assessment that asks questions like "How comfortable are you with setting up a style sheet in Word?" "Do you know how to send blind carbon copies in Outlook?") These pre-assessments help you determine if a session is aimed at the right level for your learner. Ask the target person to answer the questions and have his/her boss answer them based on their experience of observing the person. (Obviously, the boss won't be able to answer all the questions.)

The boss and the target attendee should jointly decide if a session would be worth taking, and decide on some ways the attendee can demonstrate new competencies when returning to work.

The most valuable programs will have built-in accountabilities, follow up, and pre- and post-session measures. You're probably only going to get these on custom-designed programs for your specific organization. And yes, it will cost more than sending someone to a one- or two-day session. But you will get far more ROI if the program is built to include all the right pieces for sustained learning.

It's like buying a house. You could buy a pre-assembled home that has a roof, floor, walls, kitchen, bathroom, etc. and would be inhabitable. Or, you could custom build a house that you know is going to give you exactly what you want for the long term. The latter will take some time and thought, and costs more, but it doesn't have to take your life savings. And you will probably be a lot happier with something that is built around your specific wants/needs. And working with the architect or builder you can make modifications along the way that will ensure you'll get what you want to be happy.

2. How do I pick the training options that are most relevant? Which training will impact my business/department the most?

Here are some questions to ask yourself and your senior team:

▲ Which skills could add value to our bottom line — sales, technology, management?

▲ Where are we having the most problems — management, communication, customer service, project management?

▲ In what areas do our key people need to grow to get us to our 6-month, 1-year, 2-year goals? Finance, sales, marketing, management, technical skills?

Put your focus, time and money toward the most critical of these issues.

3. *How can I justify the cost of training (ROI)? How can we track training results?*

You justify the cost of any development effort by measuring the areas for improvement before and after that effort, then 6 months afterward. Always be raising the bar for yourself and your staff to perform more effectively.

Measurable results can include:

▲ Reduced turnover per organization and manager

▲ Increase in promotions per managers' department

▲ Reduced scrap/rework

▲ Reduced customer complaints

▲ Higher customer satisfaction ratings per person and/or department and/or shift

▲ Fewer grievances

▲ More sales per person/department/shift

▲ Higher profit margin

▲ Higher percentage of quotes/bids/RFPs accepted

▲ Fewer lost customers

▲ More new customers

▲ Higher average profit per employee or customer

▲ Higher average or actual revenue per employee or customer

▲ Increased repeat business

▲ Reduced absenteeism

▲ Reduced injuries/higher safety record

4. *How can I have a plan to develop my people (create a career path)?*

Start with assessing the individual's current strengths and areas of needed improvement (use a 360-degree feedback tool, or something similar). Then decide where s/he and you want these skill levels to be in 6 months, 1 year, 2 years. Where is the gap? How do they need to perform differently to step up to new responsibilities or keep growing with the company?

In partnership with the target person/group, determine some ways to help them get there. A mentor/coach might be appropriate, or a long-term development program, or some specialized classes, with accountability to show integration of the new skills/knowledge.

All growth paths do not need to lead to management. Have a non-management growth path. Individual contributors can grow within their class without having to take on management responsibilities. Many don't want those responsibilities, but think that's the only career growth plan available.

5. How can I (or someone in my company) think like a training manager?

Actually, I usually talk to training mangers about how to think like a CEO! CEOs are bigger-picture, long-term strategic thinkers, while training managers are often short-term, tactical thinkers. So take your natural inclination, long-term, strategic thinking, and apply it to your best resource — people. Write your answers to these questions:

▲ Who do we need to be working here in 6 months, 12 months, 2 years to get us to our goals? (Think skills, not names of individuals.)

▲ What are the skills, talents, knowledge and attitudes we need to have in place now to get us where we need to be?

▲ What are the skills, talents, knowledge and attitudes we need to have present at each of the 6-month milestones?

▲ Where are the gaps with the skills and talent we currently have and where we want to be?

▲ Who would be the candidates to start with, who are most receptive and hungry for opportunity? Who would we start with to give us the best return from the investment in their growth?

▲ How will we know our people are acquiring the skills to get us to our goals? What benchmarks can we look at to determine this (see measures from previous question)?

▲ How can we grow our people to the next level? What's our plan? Who can we get to come help us design the best route, and make this manageable?

▲ What are we willing to invest to grow our people and company?

6. *What should be the role of the CEO or department head in training/development?*

▲ Be a role model. Always be working on your own processes, skills, knowledge, and practices. Don't just give learning lip service. Find ways to enhance your own skills, not by taking a "seminar" which is really just a golf outing. Be committed to your own continuous improvement by seriously working on yourself. Hire a coach/mentor.

▲ Be a cheerleader. Challenge others to constantly be improving. Offer coaching/mentoring to your key talent. Notice when people are trying new skills, even if they aren't good at it yet. Compliment their efforts. Read — and have your managers read — "A Manager's Gardening Guide to Growing People" on page 21.

▲ Show up for in-house training, even if it's just to kick it off. Your presence says volumes about the importance of this development effort. Say a few words on why the participants' attendance is important to you, the company, and to them. Say what you expect to see shift as a result of their implementing the ideas in this program, and how you're going to look for those who really take on applying new skills and ideas. Read "How to Get the Biggest ROI from Your Department Training" on page 37.

▲ Make your staff (and yourself) accountable for improving themselves and their team. To know how to do this, read "The Three-Legged Stool for Training Success" at on page 33.

Developing your key talent takes thought, planning, time, effort and some money. But the alternative — not developing your key staff — may kill your business. Don't put off this important effort just because it may not seem urgent.

8-Step Process for Creating a More Effective Workforce

A more effective workforce is created by continual personal and organizational improvement. This comes from having individuals constantly looking for ways to work smarter — both individually and organizationally. These improvement efforts are often spawned from professional development activities that not only force them to examine their own processes, but provide tools and skills for implementation.

Long-lasting professional development does not come cheaply or without thoughtful effort. But the alternatives — none or poorly conceived and executed activities — can cost many times more. For you to get the highest ROI, many elements need to be determined — from determining clear, achievable objectives, to a plan for reinforcement.

Based on more than 25 years in the professional development field, I've seen some programs that worked, and many that didn't. I don't want you to waste your time or money so I developed an 8-step process to ensure success.

1.   Clarify your desired outcomes

Determine what you're trying to accomplish: Leadership succession? A more customer-focused staff? A more cohesive team? Better functioning managers? Fewer customer complaints? More revenue per person or customer? Where do you want your people performing in 3, 6, 12 and 24 months?

What restrictions must be considered? Is the culture one of resistance to change? Does the culture encourage — or sabotage — professional growth? How is professional development fostered? How are training opportunities determined? What other development methods are employed? How are the new skills nurtured and reinforced? How does the organization support time for development? How is individual professional development tracked and rewarded?

It's critical to identify the desired outcomes and possible restrictions for any project and how you will know if the effort is successful.

2.   Identify gaps

What is the performance of the group or individuals now? What do you want it to be? What performance measures are in place now? Are they sufficient? Are they really measuring the appropriate outcomes or do you need to put new metrics in place? How and what measures will be gathered before the plan is launched?

Establish key ways to measure improvement in the target group's or individual's behavior. How will you see the results of the new or strengthened skills and behaviors? How often will this be measured?

If your people aren't performing as you want, why not? What gets in their way? Is it a skill issue or a motivation issue? What is your plan to close the gap? Gather feedback on each person's performance via a 360-degree assessment or other methods and build individual development plans.

3. *Streamline individual &organizational processes*

Individuals' performance is often hamstrung by ineffective organizational processes. First, look at how the organization's practices get in the way of optimal individual performance. Reduce the roadblocks for success. Then focus on enhancing each key of your talents' skill sets and making their personal processes most effective.

Are there organizational roadblocks that prevent your people from accomplishing more? Are there processes that haven't been challenged in years — or decades? Are your people incented to come up with new ways of working smarter?

How do you know if your organizational processes are helping or hindering productivity? We ask questions and help you challenge the status quo. We help you identify barriers and work through solutions with other departments or suppliers.

4. Enhance target group's skills

Determine how the target group's skills are best enhanced — if group or individual learning processes are better. If group sessions are optimal, offer optional self-study resources for those needing/wanting more development outside the group sessions. Create appropriate delivery mechanisms based on the needs of the target group (e.g., in-person group seminars, manager-led structured discussion guides for team training, teleseminars for remote groups, group video-learning coupled with discussion, individual study with manager, e-learning, tests for ability to apply information).

5. Increase individual's productivity

Adults learn through application and repetition. One-time hits of a learning experience are not nearly as valuable as a longer-term approach, with checking for understanding and application, then reinforcement. For longer-lasting results and higher ROI, development must take place over time.

Some ways to increase individual learning — and therefore productivity — include short learning experiences every other week, 30-minute manager-led discussions at staff meeting, 1-hour teleseminars every other week, 1-hour group video-learning brown bag lunch sessions, one-on-one coaching. This allows participants to apply key concepts regularly, rather than one long 1- to 5-day program with minimal application and impact.

Follow-up/reinforcement is critical to long-lasting development. With the target audiences' manager(s) outline a plan for internal coaching and feedback sessions. This could include bi-weekly individual coaching of participants, monthly teleseminars with all participants, quarterly in-person refreshers, or 6-month 360 feedback to determine if behaviors have changed.

6. Measure results

Measurement is key. Create benchmarks to let you know if what you are doing is working and with whom. Plan to make adjustments along the way.

7. Boost profits

Profits should increase as a result of increased effectiveness. Make sure that is one of the measurements that gets integrated into the metrics.

8. Celebrate success

Hard work deserves celebration. No effort is perfect, so celebrate successes along the way.

Training sessions can yield remarkable developmental results – or few – depending on how the trainee's manager supports the training.

A Manager's Gardening Guide to Growing People

Growing people is like gardening — given the right circumstances, people, like plants, will grow and flourish. But, like an ill-planned or neglected garden, people, without proper development can fail. Training sessions can yield remarkable developmental results – or few – depending on how the trainee's manager supports the training.

After nearly 30 years in the people-development business, and 30 years as an avid gardener, I began to see the parallels. This epiphany happened in the garden, of course! Before sending any of your staff to training, consider the ideas in this guide to cultivating people.

	Gardening	*Managing People*
	Prepare the soil. Remove any rocks or obstacles. If the earth isn't tilled and augmented, the seeds will not sprout, will be stunted, or will die.	Prepare the environment. Make sure learners have coverage for their responsibilities so they won't be interrupted during sessions. Appoint someone else to respond to questions while the learner is focusing on learning.
	Don't just scatter the seeds. Scattering the seeds on top of unprepared soil means 95% of the seeds will get eaten by birds and bugs, or not sprout. For better success, sow the seeds carefully, then cover with rich earth.	When anyone can self-select a course based on what they think might be useful, the results may be unhappy participants, managers and training departments. With no preparation, careful selection and follow up, most training is a waste of time.

	Gardening	Managing People
	Select the right plant. A redwood won't grow well in a small space. Ground cover won't become a tree. Understand what you want and choose the best plant for the job.	Select the right learner. If someone doesn't like people, no amount of training is going to turn him into a stellar customer service rep. Make sure you are not trying to fix someone's personality by sending them to training. Instead, perhaps s/he needs a transfer or other duties.
	Be clear on your expected outcomes. If you want ample tomatoes to make pasta sauce, you'll need to plant enough plants to yield abundant fruit. If you've had sufficient yields with a certain variety, you can expect similar results again.	What do you want to happen as a result of this development experience? For the learner to be a better presenter, make more sales, accomplish more? How will you measure their performance before and after the experience to determine if the effort was a success?

	Gardening	Managing People
	Plant in the right season. Each plant has certain circumstances that make it grow well. Planting in the wrong season will not produce healthy plants, if any at all.	Make sure the timing is good. Is this the right time for developing the learner? Will s/he be able to concentrate on learning and practicing new skills? Or is the environment too rocky (chaotic) to allow time for reflection and practice? Is s/he motivated to learn right now, or too busy fighting fires?
	Prepare the seeds/plants. Some seeds sprout best after overnight soaking. Transplants perform better with their root balls separated. Some bulbs produce the best blooms after 6 weeks of cold before planting. Knowing what your plants need and providing it produces the best results.	Prepare the learner. Determine what are the growth areas, and how can s/he best get the development they need. If a course is the best solution, the learner should list 3-5 learning objectives, and take responsibility to get what they need from the course, the instructor, or other resources.

	Gardening	Managing People
	Carefully and thoughtfully plant the seeds/plants. Don't just haphazardly throw them into the ground. Carefully place each one, gently covering them with rich soil and water.	Send learners into the experience knowing they have coverage and support from their team and manager. Their mind can't be back at their desk and in the training session.
	Fertilize, weed and water regularly. Without fertilizer, plants are stunted. Weeds can quickly overtake desired plants if unchecked. And without the right amount of water plants either drown or wilt.	Regularly reinforce and coach. Development is an ongoing activity. Until one has competency, you need to continually be conscious of weeding out old, ineffective behaviors. "Catching people doing something right" is the watchword while people are mastering new skills. Coaching to refine those new skills is critical.

	Gardening	Managing People
	Allow time to germinate. Don't expect seeds to sprout the next day after planting. It takes time for the seed to develop and take hold.	New skills don't always show up overnight. Don't send someone to a training and expect him/her to immediately use new skills. It may take a week or more for him/her to be comfortable trying something new.
	Protect from pests. Especially in the early stages, new growth is vulnerable to birds, pests and animals. You must protect your new sprouts from being devoured.	Protect your learner from criticism. A new skill is likely to not be done particularly well the first few times. When someone is trying something new, it's important that they be allowed to do it poorly at first.

	Gardening	Managing People
	Know when to transplant. If a plant isn't doing well, it may be because the sun or soil isn't right. Learn as much as you can about the plant to determine if it is time to trans-plant.	When someone isn't doing well, it might be time to give them new duties.
	Stake up when plants start to fall over. Overgrown plants need sup-port, or they can break off. Staked plants grow taller and stronger, and produce more abundant yields.	Coach and sup-port someone if they start to falter. Even after displaying competence in new skills, when people are under too much stress, they may revert back to old ways. Make sure you support them in using their more effective skills.

	Gardening	Managing People
	Celebrate the results. Enjoy the flowers and delicious fruits and vegetables. Your caring gardening has yielded delicious and appealing results.	Acknowledge positive changes and celebrate successes. A lot of work has gone into this effort, so make sure to enjoy the results.

Three Ways Managers
Approach Training

In my decades in the people development business, I've notice three common ways managers approach training. Following details each and the results.

Your Need	Method	Benefits	Drawbacks
"Compliance" fix (one your boss/organization/HR/law requires)	1-hr. to 2-day mandatory training or e-learning.	• You get to status it as accomplished. • Participants get at least some training.	• Nothing changes. • Waste of time and money. • Participants feel they don't really need the training, so resist many of its key elements.

Your Need	*Method*	*Benefits*	*Drawbacks*
"Miracle" fix	1-hr. to 2-day training, or e-learning, that you hope fixes the performance challenges of your team.	• It's short, so even if it doesn't work, your team hasn't wasted too much time. • Participants get at least some training.	• Nothing changes. • Waste of time and money. • Participants feel they don't really need the training, so resist many of its key elements.
Long-term development solution	Customized, multi-session on site training, specific to your people's needs, with pre- and post-program measurement, accountability, follow up, coaching and management involvement.	• ROI is high, because the program includes issues germane to your environment, repeated skills practice, reinforcement and coaching between	• Takes more time than a quick fix. • Takes support from and accountability to each participant's manager.

Your Need	Method	Benefits	Drawbacks
		sessions, and management involvement, which ensure new skills are being applied. • Helps retain key talent, as it is clear the organization has invested in their development. • Short 2- to 3-hour sessions, mean fewer interruptions because their team can cope for a few hours. • Time to practice the skills in and between sessions to integrate	• Can cost more than some 1- to 2-day trainings.

Most of the managers I've been approached by want a quick training fix. Unfortunately, 99% of the time it not only isn't a fix, but it's a waste of time and money.

A smarter approach is one that works — a well-planned and executed program that encompasses only the issues most useful to the target group, as well as only attended by those who need the training.

So consider what you're really wanting to accomplish, and decide which of the three methods will yield you the highest return.

The Three-Legged Stool for Training Success

The 16-session manager training program was phenomenally successful. Ninety percent of the attendees were offered promotions within a year of their graduation. Why was the program so successful? Because all of the legs on the Training Success 3-legged stool were strong.

The components of the Training Success 3-legged stool are:

▲ Learner's manage

▲ Learner

▲ Instructor/content provider

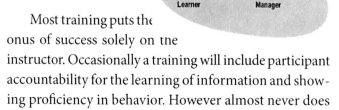

Most training puts the onus of success solely on the instructor. Occasionally a training will include participant accountability for the learning of information and showing proficiency in behavior. However almost never does any part of the responsibility for success reside with the learner's manager. But that component of the training is essential to success.

If one of the parties doesn't do their part, the stool becomes wobbly or collapses. Here are the responsibilities of each leg of the Training Success stool:

1) *The learner's manager has to:*

▲ Talk to the learner(s) before the training to determine areas of needed improvement and to ensure the identified training is the best way to acquire the needed skills and/or information.

▲ Be clear on how s/he expects the learner to perform differently as a result of the training.

▲ Co-create measures with the participant for determining if the learner successfully integrated new skills/information.

▲ Encourage the learner to take charge of his/her learning by being active in the training and getting what s/he needs from the session(s).

▲ Release the learner for training sessions, ensure s/he attends, and arrange coverage for the learner's duties while in training.

▲ Talk with his/her learner(s) regularly to discuss adapting the new skills to their department.

▲ Coach the learner when needed.

▲ Give the learner positive feedback for observed

behavior changes.

▲ Model effective behavior him/herself.

▲ Talks with the instructor regularly to get feed-back on his/her learner.

▲ Support any reinforcement offered.

2) *The learner has to:*

▲ Talk to his/her manager before the training to determine areas of needed improvement and to ensure the identified training is the best way to acquire the needed skills and/or information.

▲ Be clear on what s/he wants from the training and actively makes sure s/he gets it.

▲ Be fully committed to strengthening or learn-ing new skills.

▲ Attend the sessions and be fully involved in the discussions and processes.

▲ Actively seek real-life, job-specific application of the principles discussed/skills learned.

▲ Complete any pre-reading or homework.

▲ Accept coaching from the instructor and/or manager.

▲ Participate in any follow-on reinforcement of-fered.

3) *The instructor/content provider has to:*

▲ Provide stimulating, useful, and clear content and processes.

▲ Prepare pre- and post-learning assessments.

▲ Be approachable and open to dissenting opinions.

▲ Provide an integrated approach to learning, including job aids and practice.

▲ Create useful tools and resource materials.

▲ Give learners needed coaching/feedback.

▲ Make modifications to the program/tools when appropriate.

▲ Offer the learners' managers suggestions for coaching the learner.

How to Get the Biggest ROI from Your Department Training

Y ou have decided the best way to train your team is via a department-wide training session. This can be a smart option and can yield big dividends. But only if you have a plan for what you'll do before, during and after the session(s).

If you have invited me to work with your team, then you and I are partnering to make the training a success. By working hand-in-hand, we can ensure you get the biggest ROI from our work together. Following are some ideas to get the biggest return on time and investment.

Show the staff that you think the training is important. You do this by your words and actions.

Before:

▲ Be enthusiastic about the training

▲ Discuss with your staff why you think this training is important

▲ Meet with each team member and determine three areas you want him/her to focus on during the training.

During:

▲ Attend the training. Your presence says that this is really important. And *be* present — don't read, take cell phone calls, do paperwork or work on your laptop during the session.

▲ Participate actively — don't sit in the back or "audit" the training.

▲ However, in a small group discussion, let others take the lead. Jump in if conversation lags or they get off track. They have more buy-in when they think of the ideas.

▲ Spread out — managers shouldn't sit together.

▲ Sit with people other than your department if the training involves several departments.

▲ Be vulnerable — admit when you've done something wrong, or challenges you still face.

▲ Take notes — even if the notes are on how you'll adapt the info. to your group.

▲ Encourage others.

▲ Avoid side talk, leaving the room, coming in late.

Afterward:

▲ Within a week, discuss what each of your team plans to do differently as a result of the training. Get each person's list so you can acknowledge them when you see them practicing the new idea.

▲ Solicit your staff's ideas on how to improve on the areas the training discussed.

▲ Keep the conversation alive. At every staff meeting, take one concept from the training and reinforce it.

▲ Before a staff meeting, assign the staff to read one of my articles from www.RebeccaMorgan. com. You are welcome to use any of them that would be useful to you. Then in the staff meeting, discuss the concepts and how you can apply them to your situations. Or, better yet, subscribe to the Managers Discussion Guide Program at www.ManagersDiscussion-GuideProgram.com and get a new topic each month to discuss with your staff.

You can have ongoing development with very little time or money invested.

10 Easy Development Solutions

Developing your staff via regular events is critical to keeping them learning and improving their skills. We've developed this chart to help you see that you can have ongoing development with very little time or money invested.

Development Solutions	Approx. Cost	Your Prep Time	Delivery Time
Have each of your staff deliver a report on one of their best practices	$0	None for you 30 min. to 2 hrs. for each staff	10 min. - 1 hr.
Buy a book for all staff and read it concurrently. Discuss specific chapters and/or concepts at monthly or semi-monthly meetings.	$10-25/ person	1-? hours to read 1-? hours to create discus-sion questions	1/2 - 1 hr. to discuss

Development Solutions	Approx. Cost	Your Prep Time	Delivery Time
Rebecca puts together discussion questions for a monthly series of Axzo Press books for you to read and discuss with your staff.	$14/person, plus $300/mo.	1-? hours to read the book 15-30 min. to review questions with Rebecca	1/2 - 1 hr. to discuss
Rebecca designs a monthly series of Axzo Press Video Learning Systems with corresponding books for you to view with your staff. Each Video Learning System comes with a leaders guide with discussion questions.	video rental fee (varies), plus $14/person	1 hr. for you to review the video, leaders guide and suggested exercises in the book	60 - 90 min.
Rebecca leads a series of group 1-hour monthly teleseminar trainings with your team based on your most pressing people-productivity, customer service, or communication issues.	Varies	none	1 hour

Development Solutions	Approx. Cost	Your Prep Time	Delivery Time
Enroll in the Managers Discussion Guide Program— A conference call walks each manager through each month's module. Then the manager leads a team discussion. Each month's module includes a leaders guide and team materials. www.ManagersDiscussionGuideProgram.com	$99/ manager subscriber/month if annual subscription is purchased	30 min. via group conference call training	30-45 minutes
Rebecca leads a series of group1-hour monthly in-person discussions with your team based on your most pressing issues.	Varies	none	1 hour
Rebecca leads a series of half-day monthly in-person group customized trainings with your team, based on your most pressing people-productivity, customer service, or communication issues.	Varies	none	1-3.5 hours

Development Solutions	Approx. Cost	Your Prep Time	Delivery Time
Rebecca coaches/ mentors you to create discussions with your people and/or work on your own leadership development and/or how to coach your leaders to step up.	Varies	none	1-2 hrs/ month
Rebecca facilitates off-site retreat for leaders, entire staff, board of directors, at a local site or destination resort including spouses. Group follow-up via monthly conf. call meetings or in-person with Rebecca.	Varies	1-2 hours to create agenda w/Rebeca	1/2 day – 5 days, plus follow up/re-inforcement time.

Are You Punishing Excellence?

G ary Kurth was fired for being excellent. His performance was so great in fact, that he out earned his colleagues. That was the problem.

A story in the Santa Barbara (California) News-Press explained that Gary was among 3,400 Circuit City employees who lost their jobs in the last few weeks because their sales commissions put them well above "the market-based salary range for their role." He earned approximately $21/hour for his stellar selling of not only electronics, but the services and accessories that made the gizmos work well and easily. And he didn't upsell garbage add-ons, which meant he had a lot of repeat and referral customers.

My pal Ashliegh Brilliant wrote this about Gary:

> *Not long ago, Dorothy and I bought our first DVD player, at the local Circuit City. Having become accustomed over the years to less-than-perfect service at such establishments, we were astonished to find that the middle-aged sales assistant who waited on us was outstandingly*

good at his job. He was widely knowledgeable
about electronic devices, patient, friendly, and
very understanding of our particular concerns.
We felt we had made a wonderful discovery —
someone we would be happy to come back to for
future purchases –and I carefully noted down
his name, Gary Kurth, and his working hours at
that store.

So Circuit City is rewarding mediocrity by letting
employees stay who make within the range for their role.
And stellar sales people fall by the wayside.

What is wrong with this picture?

But before we lambaste Circuit City, examine your
own house. What do you reward? And what do you
punish?

I heard of a company who rewarded stories of failures
employees produced. No, not to encourage them to fail
willy-nilly. But to encourage experimentation, which
inevitably leads to failure. And failure, if an analysis is
done properly afterward, leads to some learning, which
leads to better ways to do it next time.

Be willing to look at how you reward excellence in
your own organization. You do reward excellence don't
you? If not, get cracking. Someone is going to be hiring
the Gary Kurth's of your organization if you don't.

Is Training Punishment for Your People?

I read an article about US Airways pilots who, because of the increase in fuel prices, were forced to take fuel-management courses if they ordered an extra few minutes of fuel for their flights. One former Continental pilot Bruce Meyer, said he had to hide that he was putting a safety cushion of fuel on board.

Then US Airways pilots took out an ad that said the airline "embarked on a program of jailintimidation to pressure your captain to reduce fuel loads." Senior pilots — those who are well aware of the vagaries of flights — were targeted for (gasp!) fuel conservation training.

Their punishment was training!

Part of this is the humiliation they felt at being senior pilots and being relegated to re-training as if they were rookies or didn't know what they were doing.

One pilot said he felt the airline was "selecting a few and hoping to intimidate the remainder of our pilot group to not add fuel when they feel they might need a little fuel. So hoping if they punish a few, the rest of the pilot group will get in line."

Again, punishment is related to training.

Do your people see training as punishment? Even if you think of it as sharpening their ax, refining their skills, reinforcing previous trainings, if they feel it's punishment it will not only be a waste of everyone's time, but will have a negative impact, not the positive one you were hoping for.

I've encountered this way too many times. Groups enter the classroom telling me they don't want to be there, it's a waste of time, they have more important things to do, their boss sent them. They start the day disengaged — arms crossed, texting on their phones, answering emails on their laptops, even reading. There is very little even a great instructor can do to turn around a group who believes they are being punished by attending forced training.

Much more successful is making training a reward for high potentials, as a chance to enhance their skills and make them more promotable. But very few managers know how to do this properly. I help my clients position training in a way that gets the maximum ROI. How they frame it to their people is important.

Of course, the airlines in the above examples, insisted that the re-training was not for disciplinary reasons. Try explaining that to the pilots with a straight face.

Who's Accountable for Personal Improvement?

Sounds like a dumb question, doesn't it? Of course, it is the individual who is responsible and accountable for improving their skills. But I've found it is not often seen that way.

Recently, a corporate group I've been telecoaching has not been showing up for their monthly calls. There have been reasons, some valid, some not. One month they had a pressing business issue to attend to. Fine, so I suggested they give me some options for rescheduling. I didn't hear back. This month the excuse was they forgot to put it on the group calendar. Again, I told them to give me some new times/dates, and nothing.

So I began to wonder, are they not getting value from our time? When we're on the call, they seem engaged and highly participatory. They say they're getting value. So what else might it be?

Accountability. Or lack there of.

It is easy to get inundated with one's everyday work so that you don't take the time to sharpen your ax. Even with pressing issues bearing down on you that you could use some input on, other deadlines take priority. So any "ax sharpening" activity, be it a coaching session or training, takes the back burner.

I called the Vice President who sponsored this coaching program to discuss the situation. He agreed with my assessment. He was going to make them accountable to their manager to report what we discussed each month and how they were going to implement it. If someone didn't show up for the call, they needed to get permission from their manager ahead of time and notify me.

So who is accountable for the implementation of new skills at your organization? If there is no accountability, I guarantee it will keep getting put off.

Are You a Good Model?

Once I used an assessment as part of a training program I conducted for a client's managers. Everyone really liked the assessment and the insights gleaned from it.

The owner of the company told me he'd like to use the assessment on everyone in his company. "Great" I replied, "I can work up a quantity discount. How many are you thinking?" He responded, "Don't bother. I got an extra one and I'll just copy it for the rest of the crew."

I was dumbfounded. I hadn't encountered anyone before who so blatantly told me they were going to rip off me and the assessment publisher. I stammered something about the assessments being copyrighted, but he waived me off with "They'll have to catch me."

Companies are usually savvy about avoiding copyright infringement. But this guy was clueless. Even if I turned him in to the publisher, he knew they wouldn't spend much time beyond a cease and desist letter to prosecute him. He was too small potatoes.

However, his employees knew he was dishonest and unscrupulous. I'd guess that's the kind of people who kept working for him, as the honest ones would move on. I'd also bet he had a good deal of employee theft as well. What goes around comes around.

Stellar Performers Start in the *Interview*

When I encounter excellent employees I wonder if they were that way when hired or if the company trained them to be that way. I've decided that it is a lot of the former, with refinements coming through the latter.

These last few weeks I've encountered excellent employees where I didn't expect them. I'll admit my bias — when I visited four rockeries to choose stone for my new patio, I didn't expect to be treated to excellent service. My project is small compared to the many big projects the rockery employees deal with every day. Yet to a person, from the counter help to the yard men, each person was friendly, attentive, helpful, and treated my basic questions with respect.

Do rockeries have some outstanding employee recognition program? Superb management? Stellar customer service training programs? I seriously doubt they have any of the above. However, they are certainly doing something right, at least from this customer's perspective.

I'd guess it has something to do with management hiring people who will fit and weeding out those who don't. Also, since the inside staff work closely together, if someone is rude or out of line, I'd guess peers and management would say something quickly.

Could they be even better with a little help? Of course, we can all improve. But if you haven't hired people with a helpful, team- and customer-oriented attitude, no amount of training in the world will make them better because they aren't open to change.

Is Being Too Nice Hurting Your Business?

I was having our monthly group consultation/coaching call with a client's managers. One brought up an issue you may relate to. He had a 5-month new staff member who has been absent and tardy too often, and has been verbally warned. The staff member had viable excuses — family deaths, personal illness, even an auto accident. But she also stretched the limits — she had to be with a friend who was in the hospital, her car wouldn't start, and she was late getting back from lunch because she got caught in traffic. Thus the verbal warning.

The supervisor was asking if he should be nice and give her some more slack, as her current absence was an unexplained illness. He had counseled her to get a diagnosis then report back so they could explore her options. Of course, she had to take the day off to see the doctor!

He was at his wits end. Her absences meant his department didn't run as smoothly as needed, but he also wanted to be compassionate to her illness.

I suggested he wait til she returned (today), get the report, then decide whether she should be put on leave of absence (with a doctor's letter), or if the doctor couldn't find anything, tell her one more absence or tardy in the next 30 days would result in her termination. (Since I'm not up on HR laws on this matter, I told him to check with his HR department first.) While it is important to be compassionate, he had come to the end of his patience and she was abusing his compassion. He had a unit to run and her frequent absences made it difficult to get the work done.

Ignore Your Counselors at Your Own Risk!

colleague called to see if I conducted seminars on Myers-Briggs, the personality assessment. I told him I've found few people who've attended Myers-Briggs who could remember anything beyond their own four-letter style. I prefer a different system, which I've found people can remember — and use — years after the session.

He agreed that Myers-Briggs was challenging and confusing, but the client was insistent. This is another case of a client "wanting what they wanted" regardless of whether the training created the results they wanted. The only reason the colleague's client wanted this system was because so many of his staff had gone through it. He wasn't asking the critical question, "How many of those who attended can remember anything about it, let alone use the information regularly?" If he asked that, the answer would, no doubt, be "very few, if any."

If you are looking for deep-impact training, explore what outcome you want and is what you're self-prescribing going to accomplish that? Or even better, engage counselors who your respect, then take their advice! You'll get a much higher ROI if you ask yourself tough questions, then are willing to be open to a different solution.

Coaching — One of the Hardest Jobs for Managers

A client called to ask me to work with her front-line supervisors. She described their weak areas that needed shoring up. As she described the litany of inadequacies, it occurred to me that no matter how much I coached them, I wasn't there to see them every day. Someone needs to be on-site to witness the unacceptable behaviors and coach them immediately, or catch them making improvements and give them positive feedback. A consultant 40 miles away was not the solution.

I had tired to convince the manager that I could work with her to coach them, or to work with her and the supervisors together, but she needed to be the one who would comment on their behaviors real time. She didn't see this as a solution. The unspoken truth was she didn't want to get involved — she wanted someone else to fix the problem.

This is natural — we all want someone else to make our problems go away. But to grow your people, you have to have be hands on. So if it is you who needs some coaching on how to coach, get it. You can work in tandem with a consultant, but you need to be involved. If you aren't, the problem won't go away. Or it will, but so will your key talent.

Prescribing Without Proper Diagnosis

A colleague wanted my input on a training program she was designing. She said she needed to design a 4-hour course on communication styles, on which I have expertise. When I asked what the client wanted the training to accomplish, she didn't know. When I asked then why a 4-hour course, she said that's what the client asked for.

The client is a manager of a manufacturing operation. He has no experience in training or development. He was unclear what he wanted the training to accomplish. So how could he decide a 4-hour course was the proper solution?

I've seen this so many times in my 26 years in the people development field. The client, who isn't clear on what s/he wants a development program to accomplish, pulls out of thin air a solution.

If you went into the doctor with a headache and said "I need an operation. I must have a brain tumor." and the doctor said "OK." it would be ludicrous. So why do we not think it's ludicrous when someone with no expertise decides on a solution?

If you want to develop your people, engage someone who knows what questions to ask you, how to uncover the critical areas for development which will yield the highest ROI, and will design a solution custom made to your situation.

Why Most Training Fails

Millions of dollars are wasted each year on ineffective training. Having been in the training and development business for over 20 years. I've seen some phenomenal results — but mostly I've seen dismal failures. The training didn't accomplish but a fraction — if that — of what it was intended to. Does that mean the training I've witnessed or dispensed was bad? Not necessarily. It means the training didn't include the components it needed to be successful.

I've seen five primary reasons training has failed:

▲ Training for the wrong reasons

▲ The wrong people are in the training

▲ No clear and measurable expectations and outcomes

▲ No participant accountability

▲ No manager direction, follow up and reinforcement

▲ Training for the wrong reasons

▲ Most often this shows up as a manager wanting to provide a training for her whole group because of one person needing it. Her rationale is "The rest of the folks could use it, too, and we don't want to embarrass the one person by sending him to training or giving him individual coaching." So she wastes her whole team's time because of the need of one person.

Instead, if the manager had conducted any pre-assessment, whether a 360, or feedback on the competency level of each team member, she would be able to prescribe training that was on-target with the part of the group who needed improvement in that topic. If only one or two people needed development in an area that was critical for their performance, an appropriate development vehicle could be prescribed. This could include sending the individual(s) to a live class, e-learning, individual coaching, or even recommending a book with the needed information.

▲ Part of the manager's performance plan has a mandate that all of his/her people "will receive training in X." If s/he wants to get a raise or bonus, all team members will sit through the training, whether they need it or not. So even exemplars in the topic have to sit in training that they could be teaching, so their boss can mark off that everyone received the training.

Wouldn't it be more productive to have the performance plan item read "All of my people will show proficiency in X by passing a test and/or demonstrating their adeptness to their manager by (date)." This would allow those already competent in this area to test out of any training, thereby saving them and the department a lot of wasted time.

Other company- or department-wide mandated training falls into this same category.

▲ Training to fix character flaws.

▲ *The wrong people are in the room*

▲ Participants are often sent by their manager because the manager thought the participant "needed help," but without the necessary frank discussion from the manager on why this development was needed. Since the participant didn't think she needed to be there, she is actively combative, or openly disengaged – reading the newspaper, working on her laptop, reading email, entering into her PDA, talking with other participants. She then rates the training poorly because she wants to punish the instructor for having to be there.

▲ High-performers who already have mastery over the concepts are mandated to attend. They are forced into training because "it will be a good refresher." They can bring down the spirit of the group because they are bored and insulted that they are required to attend.

▲ As stated in the previous section, people who were sent because their boss had an MBO that their whole team would get training in X. If there is no accountability or follow up, the participant can be as disengaged as those above.

▲ People who thought this session might be fun, or they might learn something, but without any clear analysis of what they are currently doing that is and isn't working. They show up without any clear objectives or focus, then complain that they didn't get what they were looking for. The training was a way for them to get out of the office for the day, but they had no intention on learning.

▲ People who were rewarded by their boss by being sent to a training day, as if it were a day at the spa or the beach. There is no reason for them to be there, other than they might just happen to learn something.

▲ *No clear and measurable expectations and outcomes*

▲ Often the only items measured are insignificant, like "smile sheet" scores (end of the session evaluations), and "butts in seats" numbers to show that participants came to the session. Of course people will attend most any training

— but often the wrong people will come or for the wrong reasons. And does it really matter if they liked the training? Haven't you had teachers you didn't like but from whom you learned a lot? It didn't matter to those teachers if you liked them or their teaching style, they only cared if you understood the material and could pass the course. Sometimes you learn the most from the toughest teachers.

A training director once told me the way he knew his department provided good training because participants kept coming back for more training. "It's like a restaurant," he said. "If people like it, they'll keep coming back." He naïvely missed the reality that people often go to training for all the reasons listed in the previous section. None of them have to do with training being good. Good training should yield good measurable results. But those results are not the sole responsibility of the training department or instructor, as we're discussing.

▲ People are sent to training to "become a better manager," "make better use of their time," "be better with customers." First of all, what was the evidence that they the participant wasn't already good at these things? Does the intended trainee's customers, direct reports, or other departments complain about him? Does he not produce the results he should? How would you know if he was "better" – how would you be able to observe or measure "better"? Would his work get done in a shorter amount of time? Would he reduce the complaints he receives by 25%? Would there be less turnover in his department?

Learning outcomes must be measurable – and they must be measured. Without measurable outcomes, training is a nice-to-have. How will you see the results of the new or strengthened skills? How often will the learner be measured? How will metrics be gathered before the plan is put in place?

"But it's so hard to measure the results of training." I am told. Well, you aren't looking hard enough. Yes, it is hard, but some measures need to be determined based on the expected outcomes. And each participant may have a different set of measures. Find some measures for the expected results of new or strengthened behaviors.

Sometimes a measurement of a subjective perception is adequate. For example, if Mary were given feedback in a 360 that she was not perceived as a leader, specific behavior shifts could be learned and practiced that would enable her to be show more leader-like actions. Three to six months after the training, another 360 could show if the perception of her leadership capabilities increased.

▲ *No participant accountability*

▲ Most participants come to a training event with an attitude of "I hope you teach me something I can use, or you have wasted my time" rather than one of "I am focused on learning as much as I can on X, Y and Z to be more effective." The difference may seem subtle, but it is important. In the former, the responsibility is placed on the instructor or content provider (in the case of individual study or e-learning). In the latter, the onus is on the learner.

Yes, the content provider is responsible for providing stimulating coursework. But it is a two-way process. If the learner isn't willing to learn, or expects to be entertained every minute, and to have every discussion specific to his/her needs, then very little learning will happen.

I have a theory I want to test sometime: At the first break in a day-long training, I will rate each participant on my assessment of his/her willingness and openness to learning, on the same scale as they will use to rate the course at the end of the day. Of course, the items will be different, but they would be parallel. The course evaluation may say "How stimulating was the instructor (offer useful examples, provide useful exercises, ask for observations, openly entertain questions)" and the participant evaluation would say "How stimulated was the participant to learn (e.g., did s/he adapt examples to his/her situation, participate fully in exercises, offer observations, ask questions)." My theory is that the average number I give the participant on his/her willingness to learn will match within one point the number the participant gave for the course. I believe you can't teach someone who isn't willing to learn, and they will show that near the beginning of the learning opportunity.

▲ Participants know they won't be measured on any learning, nor any application of the learning. In rare cases, they are tested at the end of the session, and even more rarely are they "passed" or "failed." They may be required to retake the training if they failed, so they are forced to sit through another whole training experience, rather than focus on the few parts that were unclear.

Even if there is a written test and they pass, it doesn't mean they can perform the needed procedures or behave appropriately in a live situation. Knowing and doing are two entirely different things.

Participants need to be clear on what they want out of the training. They — and their manager — need to be clear that this training will provide those outcomes. Expecting someone to be a stellar manager after a one-day training is ludicrous. Might he be a better delegator? Perhaps. Focus on specific, realistic outcomes.

▲ *No manager direction, follow up and reinforcement*

▲ Managers often provide training for their staff in the hopes that this few-hour event will "fix" the team members. However, team members aren't usually clear what needs to be improved, other than perhaps a nebulous "you need to communicate better," or "you need to manage your time more effectively." So they oblige the request to attend, but without clear outcomes of what is expected of them.

When they arrive back on the job, the manager — if he remembers — may ask "How was the training." "Fine" is the common response. And life goes on. The manager is then frustrated when no behaviors change. "Must not have been very good training," he surmises.

▲ It's the manager's job to set clear expectations before any training opportunity. Ideally, during a performance review, a development plan is created. Based on the needed competency improvements, a plan specific to the individual is outlined. This plan takes into account how the participant learns best, and appropriate options are discussed. If someone doesn't learn best in a classroom setting, then a book, self-study, or e-learning on some topics may be appropriate (e.g., project planning, time management). However, if the issue is not just a lack of information, but behavioral practice and modeling is involved (e.g., listening, presentation skills, giving feedback), then a live course or individual coaching is in order.

▲ Before the training, the manager then needs to discuss with the individual what she expects the learner to focus on in the training. I suggest they co-create a list of 3-5 specific outcomes, based on the training agenda. If the person were attending a time management session because he missed deadlines, these outcomes would be something like: 1) Create 2-3 ways to better track your deadlines before they are due, 2) Find 2-3 recurring items you can delegate and a plan to do so; 3) Learn how to better manage your email so you don't lose ones critical to your deliverables.

Then it is up to the individual to make sure he gets the info he needs to accomplish these objectives. If he isn't getting what he needs from the instructor in session, he needs to take the initiative to ask during the breaks, or request other resources if his needs are beyond the parameters of the course. He cannot come back to his manager with the lame excuse "The instructor didn't cover that."

Resources

Go to www.RebeccaMorgan.com to access a variety of useful resources.

Management articles

We have over 200 pages of useful articles designed to help you manage your situations better.

Managers Discussion Guide Program

This program enables you to make your staff meetings come alive in 20-30 minutes per month, with no prep by you!

Books, MP3s and learning tools

High-quality tools to help you work more effectively.

Blog

Read new ideas and stories to grow your key talent.

Ezine

Subscribe to your free copy of *Insights and Information*, our periodic ezine full of tips and new ideas.

CPSIA information can be obtained at www.ICGtesting.com
Printed in the USA
BVOW010053011112

304286BV00008B/11/P

9 781930 039278